Secrets from the Mountaintop

LIZ FE LIFESTYLE

Table of Contents

Introduction
1886

There is a sweet smell in the air. The plants are breathtakingly green. That's what I long for the most, the bright green plants that are taller than the lot of us. Looking at the atmosphere you get a feeling in your heart, a sense of calmness, that it's okay, invited even, to take a deep breath. The rain will always be there to keep the grass green. It may even become your favorite color if you stay awhile. The untouched beauty is something that you cannot explain to an American. They only know of the cities and the farmlands and the big houses. The big house people are the men and their wives who dress in suits and dresses with fine materials, strolling along the sidewalk midday. The men who are fat are the richer ones. They all started to blend together once I had stayed awhile, the big, furly mustaches, three-piece suits and tophats, and some even walked with a cane to assist them. This never made sense to me. There were no big hills or mountains that needed climbing. If their cane's primary purpose was to steady them on the flat sidewalk, then... What did Mr. Byrd say?

I am damned if I don't know. I miss the trees. The Ceibo tree, which can grow so high, you need to almost bend backwards in order to see the top. I want to climb those trees and smell the incoming rain. Here I am told that I will get my fingernails dirty if I so much as run. They do not know a thing about rain. All these men, they have raised daughters who will feel a drop of rain on their head and immediately shuffle to the nearest covering in fear that their hairdo will fragment. If Rocio were here she and I would laugh at how ridiculous these women looked, in their puffed up hair and large dresses that oddly made their skin look more translucent than if they were completely naked. It does not look like they should be wearing those dresses. They bind the women around the midsection so that their waists are thinner and breasts are pushed up, resembling some sort of hourglass figure, as I am told. Maybe it's not the clothes that are unnatural. Maybe it is the way they speak to me. Their eyes go wide and observe me from my head to my feet, searching for something wrong so they can treat me like such. They already don't like my nose; it is bigger than theirs. They seem to be fascinated by my hair. They like the thickness and its heavy weight. They ask me what products I use to make it so voluminous. I do not know how to answer such questions.

I feel a sense of dread; something bad is about to happen. I don't know why they treat me so well. They always smile intensely, and Mr. Byrd makes me talk to old men and women who have had too much wine to drink and ask me the same questions. Except, they're not really questions, mostly statements that confirm their own suspicions about me, to which I am not allowed to override. They tell me that Peru is beautiful, that is true. They tell me that I am helping them do wonderful things, that I am not so sure is true. They tell Mr. Byrd that I am well behaved. Partially true.

I want to go home. I miss Mama and Papa and Rocio. I have not come here to do what Mr. Byrd told me I was supposed to do. I am suffocated, not only in this dress but here, in America.

Mr. Byrd, I am not going to be well behaved for long.

Chapter 1
1875

Papa tells me that when Mama found out she was having me, they couldn't come up with a name, "We could not think of one that could capture our love for you. We just had to wait until we saw you for the first time."

Papa says the night of my birth was the most frightening night of his life. Mama was screaming, sweating, panting, "I wanted to take the pain away from her, I remember, I prayed, begging God to give all the pain to me. We were scared that Mama would not live after. She was very sick for weeks after you were born. You did not have a name for four weeks! Everyone called you *La Bebe.* It was like you were famous!" Mama rolled her eyes and smiled.

They decided to give me the name Lucila, meaning illumination or light. *Mi Luz,* my light. They told me that it was the perfect name for me, that they had their light to guide them through the darkness. And a darkness it was. Mama lost eight babies after me. By the time I was twelve years old, she had

succumbed to the darkness. Beneath her smile I could see that her eyes are dim. "But *mi Luz*, you are more than enough for me." I have known this is not true from an early age, because over the years, her hair has greyed more than any Mama I have ever known.

Mama and Papa liked my company. When I would spend the days with Mama, I helped her shuck corn, skin some sort of animal, make jewelry or weave, but my favorite was reading with her. Mama was a school teacher at the primary school downtown. She was everyone's favorite teacher and all the students wanted to be in Señora Quispe's class. She did not yell when a child would misbehave, instead her eyes would get very wide, and she would get very quiet. That is when Mama is scariest. When she is so angry she has nothing to say. You know you're in trouble then. Not even a smack for punishment was in Mama's taste. She believed children had to learn through experience.

Papa took me to the coca farm some days, where he picked coca plants all day long. He would ask me questions to keep my mind occupied, so I wasn't thinking about how my hands and back ached, or how the beating sun showed no mercy on my exposed skin, "When you were very young, *hija*, I used to bring you out here, and you would complain and complain until I told you to swim in the pond over there." He turned his head northward, "I always knew you were attracted to the Earth more than water. Anyways, now you stay with me."

I did play in trees and dig in dirt more than I swam in lakes like the other children. Something about pressing my bare feet against the grass after it had just rained, or climbing a steep hill when I could almost see the top, it feels like the world has gifted us a new breath, a fresh start.

One day, when I was helping Papa, I saw a man I would soon come to know as Mr. Byrd, or Sir, as Papa referred to him while navigating his broken English. Papa looked so small, so

insignificant when he stood next to the doomingly tall Mr. Byrd. He wore a white, long sleeved shirt that had buttons down the middle paired with pants that almost matched the tone of his pale skin. His shoes were a peculiar choice for this weather, for they were made out of some kind of leather. They shined as the midday sun beat down on his balding head as he spoke with Papa in his monotonous, stern voice. His face always looked like he had just eaten some bad chicken. I always thought he was a funny looking man. Maybe Papa had talked about Mr. Byrd before, but I am not sure. That day, I overheard the two of them talking. I am now grateful to Mama for teaching me some English.

"It is, eh, very advanced, yes sir."

"I would like to see it. Show me how to work it too."

"Yes, sir." Papa's 'yes's' came out sounding like 'jes,' "Jes, sir." The white men would say, poking fun. He did not retaliate, he knew there was nothing he could say. His eyes would drop to the group, his smile losing its energy. They were his superiors. He was theirs to point and prod when they were bored in this beautiful land.

One of the men was an anthropologist. His name was Edward.. I forget his family name. He wore the same outfit as Mr. Byrd, with different stitchings here and there. He accompanied Mr. Byrd to study us, how we work, eat, sleep, live. It was very odd that he was so interested in us. He said he was going to bring back his observations to England, where he would share his findings with the world. "If we are going to be famous," Mama wondered, "Shouldn't we be doing something more interesting for him to scribble in his book?"

Edward and I talked a lot. I think it was because my English was better than Papa's. I told him about the coca farm, how Papa gets up early to pick coca every day.

"Why does he pick coca?" Edward asked.

"Why why?"

"Why not cotton, or squash, or some other type of crop?"

"Papa always pick Coca. My grandfather, he pick too."

He wrote while I spoke. Sometimes before I even got the words out, it was right there, in his journal.

"Edward?" I asked one day.

"Yes?" His legs were crossed, balancing his journal on his knee, round glasses perched on the bridge of his nose, not looking up.

"You are going to England."

"Eventually, yes."

"You are telling England about me and Papa and Mama."

"Yes, that is correct."

"Are we famous?"

Edward paused. He smirked and blew air out of his nose. "In a way."

The white people who came to look at us had their own houses away from where we lived. The men like Edward lived in circular looking houses with a dark, sturdy roof and lots of windows. It looked like something we would live in, only more durable. The men like Mr. Byrd stayed in hotels and grand buildings in the cities. Though I'd never seen the buildings, I knew that it was funded from American money.

I had a lot of presumptions about America before Mr. Byrd brought me here. I knew it was where people came from all over the world to make money. I knew that the white people were doing the same thing to people with black skin as the Spanish did to us many years ago. When Mr. Byrd spoke about America, he described it to me like he was trying to hypnotize me, "America is the land of opportunity. It is the greatest country in the world. So civilized, oh! So grand. My heart aches to be back home."

His patriotism kept him going during his time in Peru. I knew he did not appreciate the natural essence, the fact that we did not have many paved roads where I lived, railroads were just beginning to become a main form of transportation, whereas in *America* it had already been there for so many more years and that way the economy has boomed and coal has become a major supply for blah blah blah..

I love some parts of America. But I don't think America loves me.

Chapter 2

1875

Mama and Papa tell me that we wouldn't be selling our coca
leaves to America if the Spanish had not found us in the first
place. Hundreds of years ago, when Spanish colonizers came to
the mountains and beat and tortured and made us into slaves,
they took our coca leaves too. They forced our people to work
and cultivate the leaves just so that they could make a fortune
for Spain and themselves. Most Incans died because they
brought diseases that we had never been exposed to before.
Mama and Papa like to think we have Incan blood. I like to
think so too.

We chew on the coca leaves to see the Earth, and I mean really
see it. When we eat the coca, the Earth becomes a mother, and
Mother wraps her arms around us and comforts and
encourages us to help her grow and flourish. We see things for
how they really are. When the Spanish came and made our
ancestors work in the fields, they would chew on the coca
leaves to endure the pain. The pain of losing our freedom, not
knowing what was to come of all this torture. Now, it is a

symbol of resilience, of holding onto who we are as a people. The Spanish took away millions of lives, but our identity lives on.

The coca plant was used for rituals and ceremonies. The Incas would use the leaves as offerings to the Gods, in exchange for health and wellness among their communities. It also was a form of currency; when a man asked for a woman's hand in marriage, the man would give the woman's family coca leaves as payment. We give to the coca, they give back. Those that lived in our region of the Andes mountains hundreds of years ago traveled to the rainforest at a lower elevation in order to successfully grow coca. Coca cannot grow when there is frost in the air, it needs consistent rainfall and a warmer climate in order to cultivate. We sacrificed for the coca, and in return, the coca gives us culture.

You can imagine how the Incas would feel about how Mr. Byrd and his friends are using our coca leaves today. Grinding the coca leaves, turning it into a powdered substance called cocaine. Yes, we traded coca leaves long ago, but that was for other South American nations. We wanted them to enjoy the properties. Once it reached America, they were exploited. There isn't a relationship between the plant and human anymore. But the day the coca plant truly died was the day I met John Stith Pemberton.

Mr. Byrd worked for the Coca-Cola Company, which I was told was a growing business in America, "It has excellent potential. We are going to make millions. Millions!" Mr. Byrd would tell the other white men. Mr. Pemberton apparently was inspecting coca farms in Peru to do business with. He had heard of coca and its remedies, and came to see for himself what the big deal was. What I didn't understand at the time, however, was why he introduced himself to me. I knew he was an important man, but I was rather confused when Mama told me there was a man to see me and ask me a few questions. I was in my bedroom, reading a fairytale, when I heard Mama's footsteps

lightly scattering up the stairs and enter the room.

"*Mi hija*, there is a man here to see you."

"Who?"

"He is a white man. He said his name is John Pemberton, and he wants to ask you questions about Papa working on the coca farm." Mama was visibly nervous. She spoke slowly and clearly, aware that this was a difficult situation to navigate.

"I think it's best if you answer his questions. I'll be right there beside you the whole time."

I stood up, puzzled, wondering what questions he would have for me, a nine-year old farmer's daughter. As Mama and I slowly walked down the stairs, I stared at Mr. Pemberton. He too wore a fancy suit, but he had kind eyes and a big grin on his face. Not like Mr. Byrd, who was uneasy to look at. His beard reached down to the bottom of his neck, combed and well taken care of. A man of early to mid-thirties, he seemed eager and even excited. That made Mama more nervous.

"Hello, Miss Luciana. I am John Pemberton, it is so nice to finally meet you." He extended his right hand. I loosely took it, knowing that my palms were sweaty.

"I have heard so much about you. It seems that you know a lot about the farm where your father works." He motioned to the table in the dining room to sit. I led the way, then Mama, then Mr. Pemberton.

"What a lovely dining room. So, exotic." He paused to take a look around, inhaled, then continued.

"Do you speak English?" He asked Mama.

"Yes." She replied quietly, studying him.

"Does she?" He pointed at me and nonchalantly leaned on the table.

"Some. She is still learning."

"Wonderful. Nothing like shaping young minds, eh?" He chuckled and tried to catch Mama's eyes in agreement. She did not reciprocate. There was an awkward silence that lingered in the air for quite some time. Finally, Pemberton cleared his throat.

"I hoped to come here to ask a kind favor from your family in return for some, erm, gifts. You see, I am a war veteran. There are many injured soldiers, like myself, who have pain that won't go away from the crap those doctors give us. I needed to find something that would heal not only our physical injuries, but our souls. Anyways, you're probably wondering why I traveled to come see you, Miss Lucila."

He came all this way to see me?

"Well, I'll tell you. I have been eyeing the coca leaf for quite some time. I know you have quite a relationship with Mr. Byrd, so I trust that he and I have the same vision for this project. You have worked with your father on the coca farm since you were a small child, correct?"

I nodded.

"And you are knowledgable about the inner workings of farm technology and irrigation?"

Mama had to translate that one to me. Another nod.

"We want to make a medicine that will help people and bring that spark back to life in America. I am creating a drink that will contain particles of the coca plant, but I am having trouble selling the idea. Big money men don't want to hear how great the product is from me, for I am merely an outsider on the subject of the matter. But, you, Lucila, you know about the cultivation of coca, the properties, the benefits, what your people use it for and how you use it. The anthropologist has highly recommended you to me."

Oh yeah. Edward. Thanks a lot.

"If we took a young, knowledgable, native girl of the region to write letters to the bigwigs, we could really convince them to sell this idea. Who knows, you may even become a celebrity. We could bring you to Atlanta and really show them what-"

"No." Mama interrupted.

"No harm will come to your daughter, ma'am, I can assure you of that. I will also be willing to pay her for her time. She can write them here, with the guidance of Mr. Byrd."

"No traveling to America." Her tone was cold, solid. She spoke to Pemberton the same way she spoke to naughty schoolchildren who misbehaved.

"Okay. We can cross that bridge when we get to it. The idea is very immature. We are still in the beginning stages of manufacturing. We have already bought the coca, but we just need a little push to get it through. I think Lucila can really help. I'd be willing to pay three dollars a week for her work. I don't know what that translates for your currency, but I can translate it to silver or gold if you like."

Based on Mama's reaction, that was a great deal of money being offered. I didn't think we were poor, our houses looked the same as everyone else's, we always had enough food and clothes, but maybe none of us here were rich.

"Ma'am?"

Mama was deep in thought, "Yes?"

"I should probably also mention your husband has already agreed."

When Papa came home later that night they talked in their bedroom for a long time. I pretended to read at the table, but secretly I tried to overhear their conversation. They yelled a lot. After what seemed like hours, it finally got quiet. Mama and Papa sat me down.

"*Mi hija,* what do you think of all this?" Papa asked.

"I don't know. Why does he want my help?"

"He wants to exploit little girls like you to make fortunes for himself." Mama uttered.

"Not if she stays anonymous."

"This is a trick. I do not believe a word coming out of that greedy mouth."

"This could be a life changing opportunity. If she does it long enough, you could quit teaching and we could buy our own land, and be comfortable for the rest of our lives. Hell, Lucila and Lucila's children would be comfortable for the rest of their lives."

"You sound just like him."

"I can do it." Mama and Papa quickly averted their gaze to me. Mama looked shocked, Papa proud. "We could be rich?"

"More than you could ever imagine." Papa grinned.

Chapter 3
1876

The letters were fairly easy to write. I was basically writing the same messages over and over again. Apparently I was trying to persuade the rich men to give in, or as Pemberton repeatedly exclaimed, "No one would say no to a child!" I wrote about the coca leaf, how it feels when we chew it, how it heals. I told them my knowledge of the irrigation methods used to water the coca, along with how hard my father and the other farmers work to pick them. I drew pictures of the mountains, the coca plants, and my family and I. Pemberton says this gave the letters a child-like essence that would appeal to the investors' emotional side.

Pemberton expected twenty letters a week. I delivered the letters to Mr. Byrd every Friday. My best friend, Rocio, would help me sometimes, though Papa was adamant that I not tell her I am being paid for this. "When there is money involved, people start asking you for things. Your friends become leeches that only ask for money. There is no character or loyalty involved." I didn't tell her, even though I knew her family was much poorer than ours.

Rocio's Mama and my Mama went to school together as teenagers. When Mama went to school to become a teacher, Rocio's Mama, Isabel, got married and had Rocio very young. She used to be very beautiful, as I am told. I think she is still beautiful, even though her years are marked on her face, with crinkles running along the sides of her eyes when she smiles, and smile lines to show that she has smiled a lot over the years. I think Rocio looked a lot like her. While Mama and Isabel have drifted apart over the years, Rocio and I remained close until I went to America. Rocio reminded me of a wild animal; messy hair that she never brushed and wide eyes that never could seem to look at one thing for more than a few seconds. And yet, all the boys at school loved her. They invited her to play with them after school, something a girl never gets invited to do unless they're really special. When they would playfully tease, she would hit them back with a remark so clever and quick it would shut them up until the next opportunity.

Rocio has always asked questions fearlessly. She was never scared she would sound stupid, or ask the wrong thing. "Why are we doing this? I hate writing."

"It is for a project. I am helping Papa with the coca farm." I lied.

"Why does he need your help? You don't know." I had to think about this logically.

"If I can help him with the water, he will get a promotion, and he will be rich."

"Huh." She didn't inquire any more after that.

Pemberton went back to Georgia after a few weeks. The money began to roll in, which made Papa ecstatic, but Mama uneasy. The hardest part for the both of them was not telling anybody. 20

The farmers that worked with Papa already didn't like Mr. Byrd and Pemberton. They hated that they had to respect them, that they were their superiors. Foreigners, who didn't even bother to learn anything about them or the culture. If they found out Papa was taking money from them to support their cause, it would be a total disaster.

Because I had to keep writing new material, I learned more and more about the science behind agriculture. I went to Papa's farm more often, where Papa and Mr. Byrd showed me how to extract water from the mountaintops and deliver it to the crops. I learned about the medicinal properties of coca, and why Americans were using it to soothe their pain, physical and psychological. Once the coca plant was cultivated, the leaves are picked and sent for extraction. There, they use chemicals such as sulphuric acid, calcium carbonate, and kerosene to form the leaves into a liquid substance. Then, they funnel the product into boiling water, where they add more sulphuric acid, which forms a coca base paste. With that, they add potassium permangate. Then, they begin the crystallization, with adding ammonium hydroxide, acetone, and hydrochloric acid. They then form it into a powder using phenacetin and levamisole. This is what Americans are after.

I don't think a lot of coca farmers knew what was actually going on with their coca plants, to be perfectly honest. All they knew was that white men took the plants and shipped them to America. They could have given them the benefit of the doubt and assumed that Americans just wanted to experience the properties that we valued so much. But, these were not men with hearts of gold. They knew that whatever they were doing, they were making money out of it.

A few years went by. Pemberton came back once or twice a year, to visit me, to visit the coca farm, to see how things were going. With each visit he got fatter. He would bring my family gifts from America. A dress for Mama, suits and hats for Papa, and dolls or books for me. As I grew older, the books contained²²

more complex material, as my English was better with every visit. He wanted me to study pharmacology or agriculture, as this would help build his case with investors. Mama eventually started to let her guard down, and even invited him over for dinner a few times, "How kind of you, Mrs. Quispe. Sadly, I have to meet with my men in the city tonight. But, I will remember your offer fondly." Mama never let the outside world see her American dresses.

1881

When I was fifteen years old, I had studied every aspect of farming science. Its technology, agriculture, engineering, biology, you name it, I've read it. I continued to write letters to the men in America, and they finally began to write me back. The progression from elementary level English with scribbles of the mountains and nature evolved into intellectual arguments that debated the effectiveness of current farming techniques in Peru. Even Pemberton was impressed. By this time, we had obtained quite a sum of money. I wanted to go to college, but the only university available was the National University of San Marcos. No women attended the school, and my parents did not want me to be the only girl attending.

Pemberton arrived at the coca farm in the middle of December one year. The weather was warm enough so that Pemberton constantly had a shining forehead full of sweat. It had been several months since I saw him last.

"Your letters are far exceeding expectations. You know, you're very bright. It's sad to see that you are unable to continue your education here."

"I want to. But my mother and father forbid me to go to the university. There are no girls that attend."

"There are other options." He sat back into his chair and stroked his beard. He looked at me thoughtfully.

"Like what?"

"You could go to school in America."

"I couldn't."

"You absolutely could, and should. Do you know where all your letters go? Engineers, biologists, some of the most prestigious scientists in the state of Georgia. I could ask them to recommend you to a women's college. They are all impressed by you, Lucila." *The Americans think I'm smart.*

"Mama and Papa would never agree." *Please convince them.*

"Let me handle that. You just focus on these." He tapped the desk next to my stack of letters. "You've been doing this for what, five, six, years now? It's time to move on and do something bigger." *How come he keeps coming back then?*

"Can I ask you a question?" I felt nervous.

"Yes?" He folded his hands on top of his big belly.

"Why is this taking so long? Why do I write letters for years, but there is no progress?" I held my breath. I knew not to cross these men, that they were so powerful that they could do anything they wanted and no one here could interfere with their actions. My question lingered in the air for a second. I wanted to take it back.

"Well, Lucila, you see, we are trying to develop a product that will help people. Some people are okay with the status quo. Me? I am trying to defy limits. We want this to be revolutionary. It's only a matter of time."

I didn't push it any further. But I wasn't completely convinced. If he was going to take me to America, to send me to college, who was I to question my silly little letters?

There was no talk about college in America for a long time. Pemberton went back to Georgia, as usual. I continued to write letters. One Friday, I went to Mr. Byrd's office.

"There's a letter for you from an old friend." Usually scientists would write back, but, from a friend? I assumed it was Pemberton. Mr. Byrd handed the letter to me. It was from Edward. He left to go back to England some time ago. I never knew what came of his research. Apparently, he was an important figure in the anthropology world, and his piece, "Secrets from the Mountaintop: The Ethnography of Coca in the Andes Mountains."

"It's from Edward." I muttered, glossing over the words amidst the stack of papers.

I didn't hear what Mr. Byrd said after that. Probably muttered something unintelligible or asked a question with a stupid answer. I said my goodbyes and rushed home as inconspicuously as possible. There was a note attached to the title page:

> To the star that brought light to England,

This country has fallen madly in love with Lucila Quispe. Soon, America will too. Keep up the good work.

> Sincerely,
> Dr. Edward Harrison

His report was seventy pages long. He wrote about farmers' lives in Peru, how the environment impacts our psychological state. He calls it 'eco-psychology,' where we think in terms of the Earth, and if we help the Earth, we remain in a productive and happy mental state. His parts about me were eye-opening. He described me as a "gifted young indigenous girl who contained more knowledge in her nine year-old brain than she led on." I was smart, mischievous, methodological. I had never knew this about myself. Apparently he sent this to an anthropological association some time ago, word spread, he won an award, and they soon figured out that I had authored the letters. Edward had influenced the scientists to write me back, not Pemberton. A feeling of shock ran through my body. What has Pemberton been doing all this time?

I didn't show Mama or Papa Edward's report for a long time.

Chapter 4
1882

I once dreamt that I was in the middle of the rainforest. There are certain limitations to where we can go, you see, because of wild animals and poisonous plants. I was barefoot, wearing an old nightgown that I had been meaning to get rid of for quite some time. It was from when I was young, it is too small now. Mama said boys were going to start looking at me differently, that men were too. She warned me about the dangers of men, as they are stronger, and more inclined to hurt me. Do not go walking late at night alone. "Keep this with you." She handed me a small knife. Just in case.

In my dream I ventured through the woods, looking for a way out. It was dark, and I had no weapons to protect myself. I came across a large snake, an anaconda of some sort. It stared at me for awhile, possible contemplating whether to kill me or let me be. He decided I wasn't worth it and slithered away.

Papa studied English everyday with Mama. He wanted to better communicate with Mr. Byrd and his men, so that they wouldn't laugh at him anymore. Now that money was no longer an issue, he decided he was going to buy property downtown, and open up a small inn outside of Lima. Times at the farm had become dire; they wanted more coca in a shorter amount of time with no extra pay. Papa decided he had had enough. He wasn't in the financial situation his colleagues were. He had money, damnit! Mama could have quit teaching, but she did not want to. "Besides my family and teaching, I would be bored out of my mind for the rest of my days." She loved her job, and couldn't let the children down. She had taken up dressmaking, taking lessons from one of her classmates' mothers, who was a seamstress. She was fairly new, but the foundation of her skills were present. She drew inspiration from indigenous styles and combined them with the style of dress Pemberton brought from America. She was always excited to receive a new dress from him.

I remained silent regarding Pemberton, that there was a strong possibility that no investors had any interest in his coca-infused drink, and that the only thing my letters were accomplishing is showing American scientists that I could put up a fight in the case of an intellectual debate.

Things were good. Not only for us, but our community. Money was flowing, not so much that we were all rich, but businesses stayed in business, and children remained in school, and that was just fine for us. Mr. Byrd had gone back to America, which everyone was happy with, especially Mr. Byrd. I could picture him sitting in his home. I always imagined he had a big, white house with lots of windows and lots of grass around it. I pictured him sitting in a rocking chair, smoking a pipe like an old man with time to kill would do. He seemed like he always preferred his own company to that of other's.

Mama's school year ended, as did mine. That summer, I turned sixteen years old. On my birthday I invited Rocio and her family to celebrate, along with some of our neighbors and Papa's coworker's families. Mama wore a dress she had made. 29

She had become rather handy with a needle, and this dress showed her talent. The dress she debuted was a forest green, with white and yellow stripes at the hem. The waist was sinched, so that it made her thin figure more obvious. There was a big ruffle on the neckline, which was square, along with ruffled sleeves. She looked glamorous compared to the other women. Everyone, including Rocio's Mama, asked where she could have possibly went to buy a dress like that. "I made it myself." She gleamed. A few ladies asked if she could make her one, and for a fair price at that.

Papa had a great deal of fun at the party, too. Neighbors and friends brought instruments, to which he drunkenly danced to. He kept sneaking me glasses, and with each one his words would slur a little more, "Shhhhhh. Don'b tell Mama." I gave most of my portions to Rocio, whose behavior grew even wilder, if that was even possible. I had read in one of my books that drinking alcohol, especially wine, in moderation potentially contains antioxidants that can lower the risk of heart attacks and heart-related issues...

"Luceeeeeeela." Rocio called from upstairs. She was drunk.

I ran up the stairs to catch up to her. "Shhhh. You can't be so obvious. Don't tell your mother I gave you that."

"It doesn't matter. It's a party!" She threw her hands up in the air and let out a big excitatory yelp. I shoved my hand over her mouth. Her eyes opened wide and looked at me in confusion. It would have been rather funny if I wasn't so worried about getting in trouble.

"Rocio, keep it down. Are you crazy?" I led her to my bedroom, and sat her on the bed.

"I don't feel so well." And with that, she doubled over and vomited all over the floor. Some splattered on my shoes, but I was too busy thinking about how I was going to cover this up.

In the case of alcohol overdose, lay the victim down on their right side. Bend the right leg at a 90 degree angle. Take the right arm, and place it under their head. Thank you, literature.

I left Rocio in the bedroom to sleep it off. Downstairs the music was actively playing, and the energy of the party was still very much alive. My stomach rumbled. I hadn't had anything to eat all day, I was so busy. Cake. I wanted cake. Mama made the best tres leches. I found it waiting for me on the dining room table.

"*Mi Luz*, are you having a good time?" Mama waltzed up to me and gave me a kiss on the forehead.

"Very much, Mama." I had been keeping the secret about Pemberton for months. I felt horrible pretending like nothing was wrong. I wanted to tell her everything, have her comfort me as mothers do. But she was so happy, she too enjoyed the money and gifts. Not to mention her dress-making on the side. Without Pemberton, she never would have ventured into it. I knew that if I told, Mama would give it up. Papa, I wasn't so sure about. His ethics were not akin with Mama's.

"We are going outside to gather around the bonfire." I knew what was coming. Every year my family lit a fire for everyone to gather round and sing 'happy birthday' to me. People hide eggs in their pockets or in their waistbands, and whoever's birthday it is gets a dozen eggs cracked on their heads. This is usually followed by confetti throwing and song, where everyone stands in a circle and holds hands. When the music starts, we engage in *huayno*, a traditional dance where everyone stomps their feet, covered in confetti, until the floor shakes. I was not in the mood to be washing egg yolk out of my hair that night.

I start to follow Mama outside. Everyone is gathered around the fire, chatting, drinking, eating, having a wonderful time. One of our neighbors, Emilio, who works with Papa, approached me.

"Felicidades, Lucila, sixteen is a wonderful age!" He kissed Mama and me on the cheek. I smelled alcohol on his breath.

"You know, my son has taken quite a liking to you." With a glass in his hand, he pointed towards a boy who looked seventeen or eighteen. I knew him, Emilio's boy. His name was Javier. He was a year or two ahead of me in school, but left early to help his father in the fields. He was handsome, with flowy hair that drifted over his eyes, creating a mysterious character. The girls loved it when he combed his fingers through his hair to get it out of his eyes. I knew he was a ladies' man, but never paid much attention to him. Boys like that always bring trouble with them. Maybe Rocio would be more interested. He was chatting up Isabel, obviously wooing her in the way young boys flatter mothers, knowing they love all that stuff. Later, Isabel will probably say, "Have you seen that son of Emilio's? He is so handsome and charming!" I know the type. Luckily, Mama saved me.

"Oh, he is a handsome young man. Luz is so focused on her studies, and is our aspiring university student."

"Oh." Emilio said flatly. "It is good to have aspirations. Just don't get your head wrapped up in those books, or you'll never find a husband!"

Mama and I were both taken aback. "My books keep me plenty company. I assure you they won't break my heart." My eyes darted towards Javier, as to say, *do you understand what I'm saying?* That obviously threatened him. Men get defensive when their sons' character is questioned. It shows weakness, like they are not good enough to properly function in society. Same with mothers and their daughters, too. No one likes to hear faults about their children.

"Well, I know they don't allow women into San Marcos. What's the plan?"

"She's going to America." Mama blurted out. From her face I could tell that her lips spoke before her head.

"America! Well good on you, then. I wish you the best of luck. It's not easy for a Peruvian to go to America all alone, with everything going on. Maybe you can bring your American knowledge back here and make us all rich." He stuck his tongue out playfully and kissed us both on the cheek once again before walking away. *Why did Mama say that?*

"Mama..."

"I won't let men like that question your capabilities. You are the smartest person in this town, did you know that? Much smarter than me and your father. Probably smarter than the people making the laws." Did she want me to go? I had to tell her about Pemberton.

"Mama, I don't know if Pemberton will even get me in anywhere. He's not who you think he is."

She looked puzzled, but her attention quickly shifted to something over my shoulder. I turned around, and there was Rocio, standing in the doorway, vomit covering the front of her dress, with a stack of papers in her hand.

Edward's report.

She stumbled over to Mama and me. Luckily she had not captured too much attention so that the music and dancing would stop. She held up the stack of papers and murmured drunkenly, "What's this? You're famous?" She giggled. "This Edward guy has a crush on you or something."

Tears started forming in my eyes. "Rocio, give that to me." I snatched the stack away. "This was not yours to take. You

should leave."

I stormed upstairs, panicking. This changed everything. Now I'd have to tell Mama and Papa the truth, how Pemberton doesn't actually have investors on hold, how the money came easy to him because to Americans we are a savage people with no money, how I'll probably never go to America and this whole thing was for nothing. I hated Rocio for this, even if she was out of her mind drunk.

I heard a knock at the door. "Luz? What's going on?" I opened up the door, tears streaming down my face. I saw her and Papa standing there.

"I have something to tell you. It's not good."

Chapter 5

1886

America is known as the great melting pot. People from all over the world immigrate here to give their children a better life; more opportunity, freedom, what have you. They integrate successfully and each generation is happier than the next. There are plenty of jobs for everyone, not to mention the chance to grow into a more successful person. Everyone is equal, and if you work hard, you, too, can achieve the dream that is living in America.

I'm convinced that it may have started out like that, for America. The people saw new land, heard of gold found in the West, or maybe wanted to start a new life. The old ways, tsk. They were no good. Wars, discrimination, repression, that is the way of the old lands. In America, there is nothing of the sort. Us Americans, we work hard to make our money, and boy, does the money flow. Be like us! Come to America!

Unless you're like me. Unless you are not a white man. We could use immigrants, of course. For the hard labor that no one wants to do. Come to America, immigrants, to help the white men achieve the dream. Why am I even saying we? I don't belong here. I live in a cramped townhouse with other immigrant girls who want to belong, desperately. They work the jobs no one else wants to work, cleaning houses, or working in factories day after day. What do we have to do to get ahead?

A couple of decades ago they just started letting women attend college. Except, they formed a union of seven schools for women, only women. It was because the ivy leagues did not want women infiltrating their institutions. We might distract the men, make them slip up on their studies and fail out. Or worse, we could have been smarter than them. How dare we threaten their masculinity by being more intelligent in Introduction to Behavioral Psychology 1001. And a Peruvian? Forget it. I would have been tormented daily. I bet if I applied, they'd just look at my application and laugh, then throw it in some pile that is never looked at.

I think about what they're doing to my family. Papa went back to working at the farm. He had to beg to get his job back. They're working those men harder than ever. Coca has become popular here. They still put dangerous chemicals in with the coca extract to achieve some sort of high. It has been sold in wines, powder, even used for anesthetic purposes. A lot of husbands buy it for their wives who are deemed too emotional or hysterical. It calms them down, makes their behavior more mellow. It is difficult to watch, to wonder why these people are using it. I know they are not thinking about people like Papa, who wake up before dawn and pick until sundown and don't get paid nearly enough. They just want more, more, more. More medicine to help them feel good, more money to pay for fancy clothes and big houses, more land so they can watch their children and grandchildren play carelessly, knowing that their inheritance will keep them comfortable for the rest of their lives. I don't think Americans look at the world around them. They are just too busy doing more.

When Mama and Papa write, they write with style that I can't describe as apathetic or depressed. They tell me they miss me, and ask when I'm coming home in every letter. Soon, I'll be home soon. I have to complete my degree. It's what I came here to do. Just a few more years left, just a few more. I don't think my heart can take it, personally. A few years sounds like a death sentence. I have never felt so alone and helpless. I am in a country that does not accept me, even though I am part of their higher education system and receiving one of the best educations for women in the country. My heart has been left in Peru and shattered into a million pieces. All that's left to do is wait to go home.

Chapter 6
1885

Papa wrote Pemberton many letters. Mama cried for weeks.
"How could he involve my family in this criminal activity?" He
wondered many times. Pemberton did not answer any of
Papa's letters. I stopped writing letters. The money stopped
coming, too.

We tried to get on with our lives. Mama and Papa tried to
distract themselves by putting all their focus into their daily
tasks. Pemberton always seemed to linger on everyone's mind.
Life continued on as usual, the school years started again, so
Mama and I went to school and Papa to the farm. One peculiar
day I came home from school, books in hand, and found a
package at my doorstep with no return address. It was a small
box labeled FRAGILE: HANDLE WITH CARE. I wanted to shake
it to see what was inside but I restrained myself. I went inside
and set my books down on the kitchen table. I steathily snuck
past Mama, who was stirring something in the kitchen, and
Papa, reading some business literature. I ran upstairs without
saying anything and locked my bedroom door. I stared at the

package. My first thought was that it was some type of explosive from Pemberton; now that he had no more use for me he would try to get rid of me before I could have the chance to ruin his reputation. Maybe it was another message from Edward, about my apparent fame in Europe. I swiftly opened the packaging to reveal a cardboard box. I placed it against my ear. Nothing. I slowly lifted the first flap, then the second. In it was a smaller, white box. *Is this a game just to play with my head?* I pulled it out and slowly opened the white box. In it was a small glass bottle with a dark purple liquid inside. When I went to take it out of the box, I saw a note underneath.

"I created this in my own backyard. More to come from Georgia. I'm coming to Peru for the very last time in May. I hope to see you and your family."

Sincerely,

John Stith Pemberton

This is what he was trying to sell all those years. A drink, a sort of medicine. I get it now. He told me a long time ago that he had fought in the Civil War in America, hurting himself. I guess this was his remedy, his creation of a lifetime. I went downstairs to tell Mama and Papa.

They look skeptically at the bottle I presented before them. "Is it poisonous?" Papa asked.

"No, I think he actually did it. He made the medicine." I opened the cap to sniff it.

"I don't want to try it." Mama interrupted. "We don't know what sort of things he put in there."

I suddenly didn't feel angry towards Pemberton anymore. He wasn't trying to take advantage of us, the process just took a while. Maybe he forfeited communication with us because he   42 was embarrassed it wasn't working. I don't know. But I didn't have that sinking feeling in my gut anymore. I took a sip. It was good, sweet. There were hints of wine, sugar, it was almost tangy. I felt relaxed.

"It's good." I remarked. Papa tried it next. "Not bad."

Mama didn't try it. She still didn't trust Pemberton, and even worried that his money was fraudulent. After Rocio found Edward's report, word got around that we were taking money in return for favors for businessmen in America. They called us traitors to our country, a lot of times to our faces. It was an embarrassment for all of us. But after a while, when the money stopped coming, people stopped talking. It was like it never even happened.

At school, Javier approached me more and more. At first, it was because of the rumors. He tried to get information out of me so that he could be the first one to tell our peers new news. I called him a cojudo, a dumbass. He smirked and walked away.

I'd be lying if I told you I wasn't at least curious in him. After all, he was very handsome, and his father said he had an interest in me. I pictured holding his hand, brushing his floppy bangs away from his eyes... Well, he was very handsome! When you're good-looking, people treat you differently. That's probably why he is so overconfident. He'd rarely been told 'no' in his life. Add that to his charm, and you've got a dangerous combination. I never had a boyfriend before. No boy has ever told me that I was pretty, that they wanted to hold my hand. I had always been too busy with books.

I was eighteen years old when Pemberton showed his face at our doorstep. I was the one to answer the door. "Won't you come in." I opened the door further to ensure that his fatness would fit through the doorway. Mama and Papa were both out, and I was scared to be alone with him. Usually when he was at our house, one of my parents would be there as a buffer, in

case he tried something that I wasn't prepared for. He shuffled over to the dining room table, our usual meeting spot. He blotted his sweaty forehead with a handkerchief. "Every time I travel here it just gets hotter and hotter." He exhaled.

I noticed he brought a briefcase with him this time. "What is that?" I asked, pointing to it resting upwards on the floor.

"I have some news I want to discuss with you." He lifted the briefcase so that it was on the table. He flipped the little switches and opened it. "I trust that you got my package."

I nodded.

"Good. What did you think?"

"I liked it. Sweet."

"How did it make you feel?" He pulled out a pen and notepad.

"Relaxed. My thoughts were slower. If I took more I probably could have gone to sleep."

He scribbled words on the paper, "Thank you. I'm making a note of that." He placed his writing set to the side of him, "Lucila, I greatly appreciate your efforts over the last few years. I am sorry I was unable to provide for your family without notice ahead of time. But, I will make it up to you. You're too smart for your own good. Too smart for the schools here. You need a better education, one that will put your knowledge to use. Mr. Byrd may or may not have told you this, but I own J.S. Pemberton and Company of Columbus. It is a company that manufactures and imports medical technology, equipment, remedies, you name it. It has grown after I returned from the war. I am also a trustee of Atlanta Medical College. Now, only the best and brightest go to medical schools. I believe you have the willpower and knowledge to do it. Is this something that interests you?"

I nodded, sure of where he was going with this.

"Splendid. I'd like to enroll you in the fall."

My mouth dropped open a little bit. *Medical school? To be a doctor?*

"I think you would really thrive in that type of environment. Cutthroat, ambitious. You'd outsmart all those phonies who are only in there because their parents are important people. They've never worked for a goddamn thing in their life."

"I would have to talk to my parents about it." I felt butterflies in my stomach, like something great was about to happen. Or maybe it was nervousness. I know how they would react. They wouldn't have it. Sending me all the way to America, a place that is only talked about here. No one has ever traveled more than a 100 miles away from here. To go alone would, looking as I am, it would almost be a death sentence.

"Think about it. I will write you a strong letter of recommendation if you agree."

He and Mr. Byrd stayed in Peru for a couple of weeks. I avoided the subject to my parents as long as I could. Finally, one night at dinner, I worked up the courage to ask them.

"Mama, Papa, I have something important I want to ask you."

"Yes?" They said at the same time.

"Mr. Pemberton is here. In Peru. He stopped by the house a while ago. He has recommended me for medical school. In Georgia."

"Without talking to us first?" Papa looked bewildered.

"I've thought a lot about it. This is my only chance. They'd   46 never let me into San Marcos. We don't even have a medical school here. I could go to school for a few years, come back, and really change things. I could make you both proud."

Mama took my hand, "*Hija*, you already make me proud. Everyday. But, Georgia? It is so, scary. I would be scared for you."

"This is not something to take lightly." Papa warned, "You will be in danger."

"Maybe Pemberton can work something out, where I could live with other girls like me."

"Hah!" Papa exclaimed, "There are no Peruvian girls in America! They'd be crazy to go. All the immigrant girls who end up there are beaten or worked to death. Walking around, you attract twice as much attention as you would, even as just a white woman."

"I've thought about that. Pemberton said he would make sure I was safe."

"And why should I trust that bastard?"

"His business is legitimate. He's a trustee for the college. He's an esteemed doctor. He's one of the best in Georgia."

"I don't believe a word he says. No. You're not going." We stared at each other intensely for a second. I could see the fear in Papa's eyes. Losing his little girl to the country we all feared. If only he could understand what this might mean for us in the future.

"She must go," whispered Mama. "The only way she will ever continue her education is with this. We have to trust him. I don't want to, but it's the only way, the only way." She murmured.

Papa was not so convinced, "Is this because what you said to Emilio at Luz's party? That she was going to America?"

"No. This is the only way."

"Well, I won't have it. I don't care what he promised you." He stood up and left the house. Mama looked at me, "Is this what you really want?"

"Yes. This is what I want."

"Wait a little more. I'll convince him." She kissed me on the forehead and stood up, "But first I need to talk to Pemberton myself."

I don't know what happened over the next few days, but Papa's demeanor about the subject completely changed. Whether it was Mama, or Pemberton got to him, he was starting to open up to the idea. I think Pemberton worked his magic on him. He seems like a good businessman, educated, personable. He probably said something that would only work on Papa. The family was under his spell again. One day I went to Mr. Byrd's office, where Pemberton was waiting for me. I was going to tell him the great news. My parents had agreed, and I would be going to America. I walked into his office to find Pemberton and Mr. Byrd sitting on the sofa, drinking tea.

"Lucila! Please come in. Have a seat." He shut the door behind me.

"I wanted to tell you something," I sheepishly started, "My parents are letting me go to America to study."

"Wonderful! This will be excellent, not only for you, but for your family. You are going to make a huge difference here. Or, maybe you'll stay in America, who knows."

"I don't plan on staying there forever."

Mr. Byrd chimed in as if to interrupt what Pemberton was about to say, "We know that. We just want to give you the best education possible so you can help your community excel."

"I need to figure out where I'm going to live. And if we can even pay for it."

"Nonsense, child." Pemberton said, "We'll take care of all the pesky details for you. Don't worry about a thing except for your academics." They were making this easy. Too easy.

"What do you want?" I inquired.

"What do you mean?" He took a sip of his tea.

"I mean, this is too good to be true," I didn't want to ruin my chances, but I had to be sure, "What are you getting out of this? You're not just sending a poor Peruvian to medical school because you feel bad for not sending us money for years."

He raised his eyebrows and paused, thinking about what he was going to say. Oh no. This isn't good.

"Let me remind you what the situation is, mm? You never would have gotten this opportunity if it weren't for me. You were lucky I even sent you money at all. The recognition should have been enough. If you never met me, you and your family would still be poor, and you'd be popping kids out by now, always wondering what might have happened if you had been given a chance."

I finally cracked him. I knew it was all business, that I was his 'project.'

"You've agreed to go to America and that's that. You leave with Byrdie here in a month."

A month? That's not nearly enough time.

"But-" I stammered. He put his hand up to silence me, and I did not protest. I was too frightened to find out what he would do if I pushed it any further. Pemberton rose, grabbed his top hat and made a goodbye gesture that did not seem sincere. He walked out the door, and I didn't see him again until we were both in Georgia.

"He's not a bad man, just has a short temper sometimes," Mr. Byrd commented. "He cares about you deeply, and he just wants what's best for you."

"He called my family poor. He said my life was meaningless without him."

"Don't blame his words. It's the way he was raised, some people just have prejudices towards other kinds of people."

Other kinds of people? I didn't even ask Mr. Byrd what that meant. I knew. Some people don't like other kinds of people because they have different cultures, speak different languages, harbor different beliefs that white men are not familiar with. The unfamiliarity scares them, so they label us as inferior. They believe that they are the only creative species, which, from what I know about the history of white men, is very untrue. They have a knack for taking lands that aren't theirs, putting a stake in it and calling it their own. Nevermind the people who live there, of course, because they are going to help the white men make money. I bet Pemberton's family owned slaves in America before it was illegal. My heart suddenly sank, not knowing what fate lay ahead of me. Was I going to be treated like one of Pemberton's slaves? Mama and Papa had never seen Pemberton act like this, or not that I knew of.

But then, my heart sank yet again, because I knew there was no turning back. I knew that once Papa and Mama had already agreed, and Pemberton had already filled out my applications, played chum with his fellow trustees, and had arranged a place for me to live, I couldn't back out. This is too important to me, to my parents. I wondered if Pemberton was really bringing me to America to go to school at all, or if this is just some hilarious prank he planned in order to put me in my place. Still, I had no choice but to trust him. A lot of people felt the same way. By this time, the medicinal product, called Coca-Cola because of its extracts from the coca plant and the fact that it comes in the form of a beverage, was beginning to gain traction. There were some changes that had to be made to the product because it originally contained wine, which was now illegal in the United States thanks to the recent temperance legislation that was put into place in Georgia. So, they tried something new. A new powdered form of coca grew popular towards the end of the century, called cocaine. People couldn't get enough of the stuff. Doctors prescribed it as medicine, people replaced it with their morning coffee, it had become a staple in an upper-class American household. I knew the kind of stuff they put in there. It's not the same as coca. Coca itself is a natural stimulant, but the chemicals they put in cocaine should not be consumed at all. Still, Americans did as they wanted, I shouldn't have been surprised. They loved it. In fact, Pemberton knew how much they loved it, and began putting it in Coca-Cola to keep them hooked on it.

Chapter 7
1885

This day had come too soon. I woke up with tears in my eyes already, not even remotely prepared to say goodbye. I looked in the mirror, stomach growling. *Could I ever wear my hair like this again?* I felt the curves of the braids between my fingers. If they were to cut them off I would surely throw a fit. I knelt beside the bed and said a prayer.

Dear God...

Mama bursts into the room. Today would be off-kilter for all of us. My heart racing, she touched my suitcase, making sure it was the proper weight to subsidize me on this trip. I couldn't have asked for a better Mama. Her eyes were red from crying, and her hand shook terribly when I tried to take it.

"Mama," Her gaze met mine. "Everything is going to be okay. Pemberton is putting me in a house with other girls like me. I might even make a friend." I flashed a smile but all I could think about was Pemberton's strike of anger from the month before. Mama handed me a gift wrapped in blue paper with a silver bow, "Don't forget where you belong."

I had to hold my breath to prevent myself from falling apart. *This is a mistake.* But there was no turning back now. Deep breath in. "Where's Papa?" Deep breath out.

"He is downstairs. Go say your goodbyes."

Papa did not go to work that day, taking a considerable loss for me. He, too, had tears in his eyes that flowed despite that his facial muscles remained stagnant. I had to stay strong for them. My eyes felt heavy. I wanted to skip this part and get to it already. I needed to start my new life so that I could return to my old one. Uncertainty clouded the air and infiltrated my brain like pollution filling a pair of healthy lungs. I did not know what the result of this situation would entail, nor did I dare to ask half-witted questions that I already knew the answer to. I was not comfortable, probably the least comfortable I had ever been, with uncertainty. I had no one to trust, I didn't know where I was going. Pemberton told me to get on that ship and when the ship docks, I get off. That I am certain of.

Against my better judgement, I got on that ship. I dressed in black and tied my hair up like a lady I saw in a book do. I didn't want any trouble. I didn't want to be picked out in a crowd of people. I dragged my suitcase, which felt heavier with every step, to the bottom floor. I was instructed to go to Room 13, Bunk 2. I searched but could not find it. The hallways smelled of wetness and mildew. Men with tattoos and missing teeth peered at me through their rooms. I suddenly felt unsafe, and wished I was home. I went upstairs and asked a tired looking man in a uniform.

"Excuse me, sir?" I could tell that my accent was heavy, and I was half afraid he would burst out laughing, "Where is Room 13?" He struck me a cold look.

"On the second floor. Go up those stairs, and take a left. Keep walking down that hallway and you will see it."

I nodded my head in gratitude. "Thank you."

I looked around on the second floor and found Room 13. These people seemed less ornery. When I located bunk 2, I saw a white lady sitting on the bed, cradling a fussy baby in her arms. I assumed she had taken that bed so I threw my suitcase on the top one.

"Thanks, love. Would ye mind switching? I can't carry this baby up the top." I could barely understand her. I knew English, but only Pemberton's English. Her vowels had an upward intonation, like she always sounded like she was asking me a question. Her r's made a rolling sound, kind of like ours, but more from the back of the throat. She spoke too fast, but didn't seem angry, so I smiled at her and climbed up on the top bunk.

That night the waves thrashed so forcefully against the ship it felt like a slap. The boat rocked and rocked for what felt like hours. I could feel the nausea forming in my stomach, I'd have to find a bathroom fast. I climbed out of the bunk nimbly, careful enough not to wake the baby. I held myself steady in between the walls amidst the rocking. I found a room at the end of the hallway labeled "LAVATORY,", but it was too late. I hurled over and out came my soup and bread from mere hours ago. I wiped my mouth with my hand, embarrassed that I couldn't hold it in until I reached a bucket. I quickly stood up and shuffled to Room 13 before there was any fuss about it.

The next morning the vomit was still there. I don't think it mattered, though. Everyone was sick.

"Get yer paws off me baby," I heard my roommate say at breakfast, "Don't get a precious child sick."

"I brought something. To help you and your child."

"What is it?" She looked a little concerned, and I had to remind myself I was not in Peru anymore. I couldn't just walk up to strangers and give them random gifts. I could have gotten myself in a lot more trouble if she was anybody else.

"I brought something."

"You've mentioned that already, dear."

"Yes. Sorry." My cheeks turned red with embarrassment. I did not want her to see, as this showed weakness.

"Deary, is this yer first voyage?"

I nodded.

"Are ye by yerself?"

Another nod.

She clicked her tongue, "Oh, deary. I am truly sorry. It is scary out there by yerself. And so young, too."

If I had spoke the only sound that would have left me would have been a sob. I quickly handed her the herb and walked away.

Mama used to give me Verdolaga when I was sick and couldn't keep anything down. Explaining medicinal herbs to people of other nations is a tricky task. They have been fed knowledge that herbs are for voodoo and witchery, which we will then cast a spell on you once you've consumed it. It helps with sickness, or chronic pain. People take it to help with migraines, or to help their kidneys or livers function properly. I wondered if she even took it. Or if she took one look at it and realized that she didn't trust me. I probably would have if I was her.

I found her next sitting on the bunk, breastfeeding.

"You. What's your name?" She pointed at me.

"Lucila." *Was I going to get in trouble?*

"Lucila. Pretty. I tried some of that leaf. I was wary at first, but boy, do I feel better now. Better than before I had this one!"

She nudged the baby.

"It is a healing medicine. Good for you." I smiled and climbed up the bunk.

I sorted through my bag for some more. The nausea was coming back. I saw Mama's gift, unopened. I tore through the paper and opened the box inside it.

They say that homesickness is your heart being self-destructive, ripping itself apart and feeling pain just to feel something. A heart aches for the home, for that is where it is usually cherished, loved, and valued. When the tears start flowing out of your head and your brain starts to wallow in misery, the heart reacts too. I have heard of some people dying of broken hearts. Their spouses or children die, and so does their heart. It's a strange thing. I wondered often if I, too, would die of a broken heart. I wondered if I was strong enough to outlive the homesickness that pained me. When I opened the present I found a woven bracelet with thread and beads that formed a triangular design. It was the pattern of the wallpaper inside our home. In it was a note:

Mi hija,

When your heart aches for Peru, just know that your family is looking out for you through these walls. We are always with you.

Mama and Papa

Mama obviously wrote the letter, and Papa signed his name next to Mama's, but the message was clear. My heart yearned for another hug from Mama and Papa, to even just say goodnight to them again. I cried the whole next night.

I learned that the lady with the baby was from Ireland, and had boarded this ship to go to New York. Apparently her cousin had immigrated there some years ago and found other Irish folk and built a life with them.

"He lives in a neighborhood with other Irish. They're small apartments, don't get me wrong, but it's better than what I got back home."

"What do you have back home?"

"Nothing. That's what. Me mother threw me out once I told her I was pregnant with this wee one. I had to go find a life for meself."

I was one of the lucky ones. I had a family who supports me. I even had a place to stay and an education lined up for me. She hadn't told her family that she left home - they weren't speaking to her because she was an unwed mother.

"How old are you, if I may ask?"

"I'm twenty years-old, dear. But I feel forty."

She didn't look twenty. Her eyes were bloodshot and eyebags droopy from lack of sleep. From the way she talked I assumed she was already a mother, calling me 'deary.' She was only two years older than me!

"And what's yer age?"

"Eighteen."

She snorted, "Oh, we aren't so different. I would have pegged ye as a teenager. Look so young." She started to attend to her baby, who was crying. She pulled out her breast and fed it towards the infant. My cheeks turned red and looked away
.

"Why are ye going to America? I ne'er seen a girl who looks like you before in me own life."

"I am going to Georgia. To go to medical school."

I was scared she would laugh in my face. *You? Going to be a big hot shot doctor, eh? Why don't ye go back before ye embarrass herself.*

But she didn't. "Oh, that's wonderful." I was pleasantly surprised by the compliment. "You're going to be a doctor?"

"I hope to be."

She looked at my bracelet. "Well, those men, they can really try and push yer buttons. They'll make you think you don't have any power, but you do. Don't be intimidated by them. Ye got somewhere to stay?"

"Yes, the Peachtree Inn?"

"I don't know what that is. But I assume it's nice, deary." She patted my hand and gave me a tired smile. She looked down at her baby, who was suckling the nipple.

"What is your name?" I asked.

"Nellie." She giggled and snorted. In that moment, she looked so innocent, so young.

"My name is Lucila."

"Pretty. Got any meaning?"

"It means light."

"Me too!" Her face lit up. Mine's Latin. For "shining light,"
although I think me parents just picked a name that was
common and went with it.

"My parents did not name me until I was a few weeks old. They
could not find the right name for me. They said I didn't look
like any name."

Nellie giggled again, "They did a good job, yer parents. Ye look
like a Lucila."

"And you look like a Nellie."

"Maybe we can be each other's lights. For when it gets dark.
Write me letters if you ever get lonely. It can be hard all by
yerself, 'specially when yer parents are so far away."

Tears filled my eyes. I was instantly filled with hope again.
Who knew that an Irishwoman could bring back my morale?
She wrote down her name and address on a piece of paper,
tore it off, and gave it to me.

"Maybe I can come to you if we are sick."

"I will take good care of you." I paused. We both busted out in a
hoot of laughter, like two girls who had known each other
forever. I would miss Nellie dearly. I sure did not expect it, but,
God, was I grateful for her.

Days went by. We stopped in a few places in before we finally
reached Atlanta. Nellie and I hugged on the deck of the ship
before I got off. '

"You have me address. It's me cousin's house. Write me."

"Thank you, Nellie. For being a friend."

She smiled. It was the first time I noticed her two front teeth were a little crooked.

"When you lost all yer friends and family at home, stranger are what ye got."

As I walked down the rampway, onto the dock, I saw Nellie waving goodbye, cradling her baby. I blew her a kiss. She threw her head back and laughed.

I spotted Mr. Byrd in the sea of tophats and finely-made suits. Once he saw me, he smiled wearily and folded his hands.

"Look who made it." Not even a handshake. My stomach began to churn. "Follow me." He escorted me to a horse drawn carriage. I had rarely seen these in Peru but I hid my amazement at how common they were. There was even a man sitting behind the horses, directing them. He offered his hand so that I could easily climb the steps to get into the carriage.

I peered out the window. It was so, so hot. Wearing all black probably didn't help. Sweat beads dropped down my face with every trot. Mr. Byrd noticed and offered me a handkerchief, which I politely refused.

"You'll get used to it, the heat I mean. Yes, the summers are indeed brutal. But when wintertime comes around, you will be glad that you'll never have to wear a heavy coat."

I smiled and returned looking out the window. I thought about home. What they were doing, if they were thinking about me. I wondered if they knew I made it here safe. I wondered if Pemberton told them the whole truth.

"We should be arriving in about an hour." My. Byrd remarked, pulling me out from deep in thought. Great, more traveling.

And with him.

"Arriving where?" I asked.

"Peachtree Inn. I will give you a map so you can walk to the college. It should only be a quick skip away." He smiled that menacing smile that always scared me as a child. Now it just annoyed me. Maybe I was just so tired from traveling my instincts were slow to recognize danger.

As the hours went by, Mr. Byrd and I both sat opposite each other, reading our own respective books. Often I would get distracted by the business here. In Atlanta, many people seemed to have places to go. There were so many different kinds of people; vendors, well-to-do businessmen, housewives, young children, the young rich children, (you could tell) and all of them were white. I wondered if I were to walk down the street like them they would shout horrible things at me.

As we left the hustle and bustle of the city, my mind began to quiet, as did the scenery around us. Mr. Byrd pointed out what plantations belonged to whom, which did not matter much to me.

"That there is James Bifton's plantation. He used to pick cotton, but when slave-owning became illegal, he fell out of business. I hear he is trying to start anew with indigo." He clucked his tongue in disappointment. "What a shame."

He realized his mistake, or had forgotten who he was speaking to. "I mean, it is good that they are free now."

I peer back out the window. Whatever you say, Mr. Byrd. I had heard about the American Civil War, how bloody and brutal it was. I also knew that Pemberton fought for the Confederacy, the South. They wanted to keep the slaves under their control. Under their power. Until the Union won and President Lincoln freed them. I have yet to see a dark-skinned person roaming around Georgia. Maybe they all escaped to the North. Maybe I should do the same.

We arrived at a large, white house with lots of windows. The window shades matched the door, a bright red that made the bright white house look even brighter. I stepped out of the carriage and Mr. Byrd and I approached the door. He knocked three times. After a moment a short, stout lady with bright red lipstick and an updo hairstyle appeared.

"Yes?"

"This is Lucila. She will be staying with you for the term."

She looked me up and down. She did not extend her hand to shake mine.

"Yes. Well, you're in luck. The girl who was staying here last just got hitched. You can have her room."

She was wearing an apron and was partially covered in flour. I saw Mr. Byrd discretely hand here a fat envelope. She turned around and smiled at me. "Up the stairs and third door on your right, honey."

I don't know if Pemberton or Mr. Byrd had wide connections in Georgia, but no one seemed to attack me as I imagined. My roommate was quiet. She did not speak much, which I guess is better than speaking too much and too often. Or worse, she could have hated people like me and vocalized that often. But, that wasn't the case. She didn't tell me her name when I first met her, only that this was her side of the room, and that was my side. She pointed to the empty bed.

"That's yours..." *As if I was going to take the one that was already made and slept in?*

I placed my suitcase on the bed and realized I didn't have any 65 bedding. I didn't have anything except for some toiletries, clothes, shoes, and an umbrella.

"Miss Ronnie will get you some sheets and a pillow." I felt relieved. Maybe this country wasn't so unforgiving after all. My roommate laid down on her bed and faced the wall. She slept through dinner and into the next day.

Chapter 8
1885

Miss Ronnie, the one I presumed was in charge, did a lot of housework. She cooked, cleaned, and made sure us girls were taken care of. That is a lot of work for one woman to do. I thought the envelope that Mr. Byrd handed her yesterday changed her attitude greatly. That morning her lipstick was fresh, sort of a bright red-purplish color. I learned quickly that her lipstick was often smudged during the business of the day.

Our breakfast entailed of eggs, bacon, bread, coffee, orange juice, and apples. It was interesting. Not poorly tasting, I was just so accustomed to the spices and specialties that we had in Peru. Nevertheless, I woke up hungry and ate a lot. I noticed the other girls did not eat nearly as much as I did. My roommate barely touched her eggs.

"Girls, if you don't eat, you won't get through the day without becoming a mess." Miss Ronnie exclaimed.

"I can't sacrifice my figure, miss." A pretty girl with blonde hair replied with a sly smile.

Mr. Byrd arrived at the inn at nine o'clock in the morning. He was to take me to Atlanta, to see Pemberton. They wanted to discuss something, I wasn't sure what. I assumed it was important. After being helped into the carriage, Mr. Byrd got right down to business, "So, today is a very big day. Everyone has been quite giddy with excitement to meet you. We will meet Mr. Pemberton at his office in Atlanta, and we are going to a board of trustees meeting. You will meet his fellow trustees there."

"What is the meeting for?"

"For his new medicine. They have read your letters through the years. You are going to be the cultural perspective on the makings of the remedy."

"I wish I had prepared."

"Nonsense. You will be perfect." He seemed to be in a good mood.

We arrived at a large, brick infrastructure that looked carefully built. Clock towers stood at the corner of these buildings, and had a grand front entrance of grass and well curated flower gardens. Mr. Byrd opened the door for me and I followed him towards a room labeled "CONFERENCE ROOM." There stood about twenty men dressed alike in sweaters and suits, even though it felt like the sun was melting outside. Pemberton emerged from a corner of the room, smoking a pipe.

"Gentlemen, I'd like you introduce to you, the infamous Lucila Quispe." This was followed by scattered applause. I stood awkwardly, trying not to make eye contact with the group staring right at me.

"Please," he continued, "ask her any questions you have. She has traveled all the way from Peru to meet our acquaintances. She has come face-to-face with the coca plant. She knows all the science behind the cultivation of the plant. Her letters single-handedly helped us get this remedy become the most relevant topic in the pharmaceutical and chemical industry." Louder applause followed.

"Enjoy the beautiful morning, we have tea, coffee, and a wonderful breakfast display brought by our lovely secretaries. Boy, do they make our lives easier!" Light laughter. "Enjoy, my friends."

The men stared at me, but none approached. I was grateful that Mr. Byrd was by my side, something I'd never thought I'd say. One man asked, "Do you speak English?" I nodded and told him I read plenty of books from America. He did not seem impressed.

After a few minutes two men cornered me.

"Hello, Lucila. How do you like America?"

"I like it very much, sir."

"Ah!" The other man exclaimed. "Byrd, you have that one trained right. She's well behaved." I wanted to crawl into a hole.

"Yes, well, she is a bright girl. She follows directions just fine." Mr. Byrd replied.

I didn't say anything because I knew that I had no power in this situation. I remembered the way Mr. Byrd and the other white men would tease Papa, because his English wasn't very good a few years ago. I was afraid the same thing would happen to me.

"So, girl. How do you feel about the use of the coca plant in the remedy Mr. Pemberton has created?" Another man approached the group. All the men towered over me by at least a foot. I felt small physically and in all other aspects.

"I appreciate the use of the coca plant in America. It is good for business, but many people forget the cultural use of the coca plant. We chew it raw. It is like coffee, except its properties include enhancing minds and becoming more in tune with the Earth."

The man scoffed, "I know what your people use the leaf for. We are here to take it a step further, use modern technology to extract the qualities that make it so attractive to sicklies and those not of the right mind. A leaf alone does not do the trick."

"There are other herbs, in Peru, that help heal as well. Some are used especially for stomach problems, some are used for migraines, or some for sleeping. There is no need for altering what is already good."

The man was shocked. He looked at Mr. Byrd. "I would think she would be on board with this." He turned his attention back to me. "I would support this if I were you. I would hate to see your chances of becoming a doctor be nonexistent suddenly."

"Excuse us." Mr. Byrd pulled me away from the group, "What are you doing?"

"I am just speaking about the culture of coca. Why did he get so upset?"

"That man there is a huge part of this operation. You need to tell him how wonderful the medicine is, how grateful you are that they are doing business with farmers like your father, and how this will be the future of medicine."

I knew I wasn't there to share my side. They just needed a

Peruvian girl to give them permission to use what they were already exploiting. It didn't matter that I was there, I just gave them extra support and boosted their egos. This is the price to pay for medical school.

"Why am I here, then?" I prayed that Mr. Byrd would tell me that there was a reason.

"Damned if I know."

1886

I have been in the U.S. for a year. I finished my first year of medical school a month ago, with solid grades. I spend the summer days reading on the porch swing and writing letters to Mama and Papa. The first year was hard. In school, I stuck out like a sore thumb. I was the only girl enrolled in the entire institution, let alone a Peruvian girl. The men mocked my accent when I answered a question in class. The professors only took me slightly more serious than they originally would have because they knew who was paying my tuition. I attended many parties, conferences, and meetings with Pemberton. He calls me his "right hand girl." I have learned to keep my mouth shut about the truth. Whatever Pemberton is saying, is the truth. It's not entirely awful. I have met some really nice ladies at parties. They don't bother to ask me about the remedy, which I hear is growing in popularity. Sometimes I am relieved that they want to talk about more superficial things. It makes the time spent here seem more simple.

Pemberton has made quite a name for himself in the medicine realm. His 'medicine,' or shall I say beverage, is being sold at pharmacies and town stores alike. Georgia fell victim to the Temperance laws, which affected Pemberton's morale. He couldn't add wine to the mixture, so he replaced it with some sort of acid that counteracted the sweetness of the coca extract. I have to admit, it was delicious. It was rebranded as Coca-Cola. Sometimes when I would visit Atlanta I would see teenage boys handing out flyers that said "Drink Coca-Cola." It was sort of satisfying to see the product finally hit the shelves after all those years. No more letters were required of me. All that was left to do was put on a brave face for Pemberton's friends and tell them how wonderful the drink is.

Tonight I was expected to attend a charity ball. This is another thing I found funny about rich people with too much money and free time. Someone picks an organization or institution worth giving money to, i.e. orphanages, Christian missionaries, scholarships for underprivileged teenagers, etc., and all the attendees dress up in their flashiest outfits, and they hold auctions for experiences or expensive objects to raise the money. There's an unspoken rule that the person who buys the most expensive thing or spends a large sum of money goes around the room and receives many compliments about how generous they are. They boast a little, but not too much to seem like they are enjoying the attention. I wonder who it will be tonight.

At seven o'clock my carriage arrived at the inn. I was gifted a long, plain white dress with long sleeves. Pemberton instructed me to wear a vest with patterns of optical illusions in green and red colors. His wife saw it in a store and said it looked "native." I think he is starting to mix me up with the Indians. It isn't a Peruvian-looking vest, that's for sure. But, I continue to let my identity be dictated by Pemberton and his colleagues, as I braid my hair to grasp onto some individuality. My roommate is sleeping again. That's all she ever does, is sleep. Mama would have dragged me out of bed and given me chores, even if there was nothing to do, just so I wouldn't sleep so much. "You will sleep through your entire life if you keep that up." Maybe that's what she's trying to do.

"You look nice."

I turned around. Did she actually speak to me? I haven't heard a peep from her in weeks.

"Thank you. I am going to a charity ball.'"

"That sounds lovely."

And that was it. She rolled over on her bed and faced the wall once again. I wonder what happened to her to make her sleep so much.

Everytime I ride in a carriage I look out the window and watch the people working. Some are out in the fields, some sitting on their front porches just staring at their land. I like watching the children play the most, either chasing each other or playing with toys. It makes me miss home and the familiarities that come with having a family. The support, knowing that there is someone to turn to when something goes wrong, is comforting. Here, it is very obvious that I am one hundred percent on my own. When you're alone so much, you spend your days thinking ahead. I wonder a lot about what has changed when I get back to Peru. I still have three more years here. I don't know if I want to stay that long. It's only been a year and my heart aches everyday. I want to sleep all day like my roommate.

After a short ride, I arrive at a grand building with features that resemble a courthouse. I am not intimidated as I would have been a year ago. I would have searched the room for Mr. Byrd to hide behind, not that he was much comfort. Now, I have learned how to play the game. These people love a little entertainment to talk about at the breakfast table the next morning. I imagine what they say, "Oh honey, did you meet that native girl last night? She was so intelligent, and had a sense of humor, too!" And then the other would reply, "Yes, dear, maybe we should have bid on a date with her!" And then they go about their caviar or whatever it is rich people eat. Tonight I wasn't entertaining them for the sheer enjoyment, no. Tonight is going to be different.

I walk into the ballroom and absorb the buzzing energy happening. Classical music is playing, sweeping people off their feet and to the dance floor. Drinks are in hand, pipes and cigarettes, too. I lock eyes with Pemberton, and he motions me to join his conversation. A server stops me, "Excuse me? You are not allowed here."

"Yes I am."

"No, lady, you have to leave." This kid doesn't look any older than eighteen. After I'm done with him, he's out of a job for sure.

"You are probably new. It's okay, I am fairly new at this too. I know I do not fit in here, but I assure you I am meant to be here."

"I'm sorry, but we can't have your kind of people here. It's not allowed."

I saw out of the corner of my eye Pemberton moving towards us. Huffing and puffing, he brushed past me and got in the boy's face. He spoke real slow, "Son. She. Is. My. Guest."
"I'm sorry sir, but the rules-"

"Your rules are no more set in stone than these goddamn Temperance laws. Always a way around them."

"I'm sorry sir."

"Don't talk to this woman again unless you want to be out of a job tonight."

He nodded and scurried away like a scared animal. Poor kid. Just trying to do his job.

"What a way to start the evening!" Pemberton threw his hands up. "Come with me. I want to introduce you to some of my friends."

Here's how the night typically goes: I walk into some fancy venue, Pemberton and I find each other, he introduces me to some friends, we talk about how amazing the remedy is and how rich Pemberton is going to get from it, how my letters "have impressed the lot of us," and then I eat, wait for Pemberton to get drunk, and go home. Pemberton escorts me over to a middle-aged woman and whom I assume is her husband. They both showcase wide-eyed smiles, like I'm their favorite author and they're just waiting to tell me how wonderful my book is.

"Hi, Lucila, we've heard a lot about you." The wife shakes my hand. Her name is Marion.

"It's a pleasure to meet you. You can call me George." I shake his hand as well.

"I must say," Marion begins, "It is so impressive that you learned English and are attending medical school here, so far away from home."

I shake my head, "Oh, no. If Mr. Pemberton never found me, I would still be in Peru, probably helping my mother or father at work."

"Oh? And what do they do?" George asks.

"My mother is a schoolteacher and my father is a field worker on a coca farm. Actually, one of the coca farms that has supplied for Coca-Cola."

"How wonderful! John here tells us all about his trips to Peru. It sounds so, exotic." *That's always their go-to, isn't it?*

"It is very beautiful. I miss it so. I wish there was a way I could bring a piece of Peru and share it with all of you." Marion puts her hand over her heart sympathetically.

"John, are you paying this young lady for all the hard work she's done? I mean, she's helped so much."

This question made Pemberton freeze up. For the first time, I think, he doesn't know what to say, "Well, George," he cleared his throat, "She is very busy in her studies."

"Yes, but, you know how competitive the field is these days. She should be looking for outside work to make her more marketable."

"That is true, that is true." He's mumbling away. "Okay, Lucila, how about manufacturing? You could learn about how we make the drink and you could even do it yourself."

"That sounds lovely, Mr. Pemberton, thank you." *Too easy.*

"Well, that worked out well, didn't it?" I can tell that Pemberton felt forced to make that decision, that maybe he is trying to get rid of me so he doesn't feel responsible for me anymore. "And, she'll be entitled to a share of the company!" George lets out one of those hearty laughs only businessmen do, "Be careful, John, she may grow richer than the lot of us!" I notice that Pemberton is sweating more than usual.

"Excuse, me, friends." He leaves me with George and Marion. They excuse themselves, probably fearing the awkwardness lulling of conversation. I do not mind, as I do not care to speak with them anymore anyhow. I have what I want. Money to bring back to Mama and Papa, and to play Pemberton's game like he's played me all these years.

Chapter 9
1886

I've never been good at keeping secrets. One Sunday, when I was about six or seven years old, Rocio and I went to church, as we normally did every Sunday. The charity box was passed around at the end of the service, and people dropped their spare change into it. We noticed it acquired quite a large sum of money. Rocio whispered to me, "How much money do you think is in there?"

"I don't know. But we could buy so much candy with it."

Rocio developed a little smirk on her face. "Let's take it."

"No! I'll get in trouble!"

"Not all of it. Just enough to buy some candy."

So, when Mama and Isabel stayed after to talk to the fellow church-goers, Rocio and I swiped enough for a handful of candy. I didn't actually do the stealing, but I knew that as an accomplice, I was just as guilty. I felt a wave of shame as soon as we did it. I wanted to turn around and give it back, but we were already running to the candy store. We each bought a large bar of chocolate, caramels, and taffies. It was delicious. But afterwards I felt sick, partly from the candy overdose, but mainly because I felt so guilty. But neither Rocio nor I told our parents what we did.

Seeing Pemberton in his work element is like seeing a predator attack its prey. He always goes for the kill, hyperfocused and silent until there is a success. "Yes! Perfect!" He has a lot of interjections when things go right. When things go wrong, there are many grunts and "Mmphs," followed by silence. My job isn't confusing nor complicated. I work in the factory, combining chemicals until they form this paste, to which I then liquidize it through more chemicals. The coca leaf extract is implanted somewhere between the harmfulness, the only natural part of this whole process.

I am entitled to a share of the company, because it is fairly new. If it were a big corporation, I guarantee you I would have been overlooked. But, because business is fairly slow, I know the ingredients and process in which to make it, and Pemberton does not want to pay more for a white worker, I got the job. I mainly work on the weekends, now that school has started up again. It is difficult balancing readings and studying with working, but I never complain, unless I want Pemberton to lose his temper again. I'm saving up the money that I do make to send back to Mama and Papa, plus I want some new shoes. I see some of the men wear leather shoes, and the women wear softer flats. I want something in between. Something that will make people take me more seriously. I think once I save enough money, I will go shopping. I have never been shopping by myself here in fear of discrimination.

Today Pemberton is sending me to the pharmacy to restock the Coca-Cola supply. I pushed a few heavy boxes full of them down a few blocks on a cart, and receiving many confused and

disparaging looks from the townies. I arrive at Fulbrighton Pharmacy, a small, family-owned store that has few but loyal customers. Mr. Fulbrighton, the owner and whose father started the business years ago, is a mean man.

"Hello, Mr. Fulbrighton. I am here to restock Coca-Cola."

"There is no need for more. We only sold one last month."

One? How can that be? I take a look at the shelves. He's right. Only one bottle is missing from the Coca-Cola section.

"I guess people don't want it. Maybe you should tell Pemberton to work some of that native voodoo magic. Hell, maybe that'll pick business back up!" He snickers then tells me to leave. I have learned to brush those sort of comments off. That is America, after all. And many people actually have been nice to me. My roommate has never once made an insulting remark about my heritage, and the men at school stopped mocking me once I developed a reputation for answering all the questions correctly and receiving high marks on exams. Some of them even ask me for help. But being nice is not synonymous to being loved. I know I am not loved here. I am a spectacle for people to oggle at, even still. It has been a long year, with a little less than three to go.

I haul the cart back to the factory. I know that this will surely result in an outburst from Pemberton. His mood swings have been especially erratic lately. Some days he is joyful and even jolly. He talks about the future and all the money we are going to make. But some days he goes into a dark, dark place that no one can seem to dig him out of. He sits and his office and does God knows what for hours. He is silent and irritable and refuses to speak to anyone. Today is one of those days. I knock on his closed office door, blinds down. I hear a hoarse "come in" and enter.

"Hello, Lucila."

"Good morning, Mr. Pemberton. I have some bad news."

"Oh, great. What ever could it be this time?"

"Fulbrighton sold one bottle of Coca-Cola this past month. He refused to have any more restocked."

I'm bracing myself for impact. But, no violent outbursts this time. He sighs a deep sigh and puts his face in his hands. I think I heard a stifled sniffle, like he was crying.

"Lucila, sit down."

I sit down on the couch opposite from him. His office is dark, reflecting his sullen mood.

"I have put seventy dollars into this company. Over the past year, we've only made fifty. That's a significant loss. I am unsure of what to do. Nothing is working. I've tried selling it as a medicine, as a carbonated beverage, Hell, if those goddamn senators never passed that Temperance law everyone would be drunk and happy by now. And we'd be rich."

Suddenly he lets out a hearty cough and grabs his stomach in pain. He winces a few times before sitting up straight.

"Are you alright, Mr. Pemberton?"

"Ah, nothing but a little indigestion. I guess we'll stop manufacturing for the day if we're not selling anything." He lets out a small laugh.

"Go study."

I nod and leave the room, closing the door. I am worried, for the money, for Pemberton, for everything to fall apart.

As the months go by, Pemberton's mood changes from day to

day. Some days it seems like he has hope, that everything he worked so hard for would actually work out. Most days he is pessimistic, wailing about what has the world come to, we are all doomed, same old, same old. He isn't well, that I am sure of. I've tried to bring him some dried up herbs that I saved from home, but he always refuses. "I almost died in the war, I can handle a little cramp. Besides, those things are probably crawling with critters."

Suit yourself.

Mr. Byrd comes by the office sometimes with "medicine." I've heard doctors talk about the use of cocaine and its side effects. It's highly addictive and terrible for your respiratory system.

"He needs it. He's been hooked on morphine for a while now, and he says his pain is the worst it's ever been," I've overheard Mr. Byrd say, "I don't know how he affords it, he's not a rich man."

There are four points within those statements that concern me:
1) Pemberton has a raging morphine addiction.
2) He has raging stomach pains, possibly citing a terrible illness that Pemberton wanted to be kept a secret.
3) The comment on affording cocaine, which means that it is a rich person's drug. Surely the coca farmers in Peru that make the supply are being treated well and are given fair wages.
Hah! I hope Papa is getting away from that soon.
4) He is not a rich man. The business is failing. I predict that he will let people like me go first; the immigrants, women, the expendibles. But, his pride is too grand for his own good. He would die before admitting his failure, which as far as I know, might happen.

Although I hadn't spoken to him in years, I sat down to write Edward a letter.

Dear Edward,

I hope this letter finds you well, if this is still your same address. It has been quite some time, and if you haven't heard already, I am attending medical school under Pemberton's recommendation, and I guess a little bit of yours, too. Over the past few years, I have been in America helping Pemberton sell Coca-Cola to investors. He claims that I am here to provide a cultural perspective, but I am not sure that is true. In return he has supported me through medical school and given me a place to stay at a local inn. While I am very grateful, I believe that Pemberton is on the verge of death and is going to sell the rights to the company. While I am promised a share of the company, I need to collect that money and return to Peru.

Is there any way you can help me?

Your Star,

Lucila Quispe

Edward is my last hope for the money, to go home. Mr Byrd and Pemberton cannot be trusted for obvious reasons. I waited restlessly for about a month, until Miss Ronnie announced that there was a letter for me from "A man from England?! So sophisticated!"

Dear Luz,

Receiving a letter from you brought a smile to my face, then discovering that you are in peril suddenly shifted my mood. I am shocked to hear about Pemberton and his fate. But, you are right to worry. He is not one to be generous in the end. But, you must wait until the end. If he dies before he can sell the company, or vice versa, either way you will be free. In the meantime, this is all I can give you from across the Atlantic.

Enclosed is twenty dollars, enough to last me a year.

*I hope you are well, and taking care of yourself. When you see
your parents again give them my regards.*

Your friend,
Edward

Another few months pass by. Pemberton grows sicker and
sicker and eventually can't come into work anymore. I found
out it was stomach cancer that spread. I miraculously still have
a job that pays me. That combined with Edward's donation is
more than enough to get me through the year. Who knows,
maybe I could even finish school?

I'm taking off work this weekend to study for final exams. With
everything going on I'm glad that this is happening. It's
something to distract me from the possibility of my world
crumbling. While I'm in the library, a couple of young men
with thick southern accents ask for my help. It makes me feel
important, like I'm the best at something. It feels even better to
know that I'm better at them at something that isn't even in my
first language. Tutoring these men somewhat makes me feel
closer to Mama and Papa, teaching them a skill that I've
mastered. I wonder what will happen if I come home sooner
than expected.

The Monday after, I arrive at the factory expecting an empty
seat in Pemberton's office. Instead I am surprised with the
spitting image of Pemberton, except younger, thinner, and no
beard. His son, Charles. He and Mr. Byrd were chatting,
obvious that Mr. Byrd did not respect nor value Charles'
presence. I would have thought that Mr. Byrd would have been
the runner-up to Pemberton, but, family first, right?

As I'm cranking levers, putting chemicals in test tubes,
formulating acids into paste, Charles approaches me.

"You're that girl from Peru, right?"

"Yes, sir. Lucila."

"My father says you're very smart. That you're going to be a doctor."

"I'm taking classes. I'm not sure if-"

"Well, if you're smart, then you can help me with this."

He motions for me to follow him to his office. He sits down at his father's desk, which is covered with a plethora of documents.

"My father is very sick, as you know, and does not have much time left. I am reading here that you have a share in the company."

"Yes, sir." He looks my age.

"Well, from the looks of it, that's not going to happen."

I am gutted, but unfortunately not surprised.

"Why not?" I'm trying to form tears in my eyes, so he would panic at the sight of a crying girl and get her anything to stop.

"We're selling the company to one of my father's friends, another pharmacist. It's not selling for very much."

"But I've been here since the beginning. I helped even when I was barely able to speak English. I've known your father for more than a decade."

"I've known him longer. I wanted to tell you that we will be meeting with Mr. Candler to sell the business tomorrow. Plan accordingly."

He's colder than his father. If I didn't have excellent self-control, I would have pounced over this desk and clawed his eyes out. All that work, to be sold out by a man my own age? What a sick, sick, person. If this is my last day, I'm going to make it count.

"Mr. Pemberton?" I murmur on my way out.

"Yes?"

"I hope you're next."

It's time to plan my escape. I can't let Pemberton, or anyone here for that matter, know. The only people I told was Mama and Papa. I wrote them a letter telling them I'm coming home. I don't want to finish medical school anymore, there is no point. There's no way that Charles will carry on his father's promises when he's dead. He isn't holding them up while he's still alive. I walk to the Atlanta train station on June 19th, 1887. I ask for one ticket to New York City. I have to write one more letter before my departure tomorrow.

Chapter 10
1887

After dinner that night, I silently pack my things, careful not to wake my roommate. She turns over a number of times, but usually she is a pretty heavy sleeper. I wear the black outfit that I arrived in almost two years ago. That girl who arrived was so scared, so vulnerable. She is not who I am now.
I step out the front door of the inn, trekking my way to the train station. It is about a three-hour walk. I can't ask Mr. Byrd for a carriage, it would have been too conspicuous. I assure myself that I can sleep on the train, knowing that I probably won't. My heart is pounding at the thought of being caught. I only brought what I could carry, leaving a majority of my clothes to my roommate. I hope she will appreciate the gift and not consider it a burden.

After a long walk I arrive at the train station around sunrise. My train stops, and I get on board. I bought the cheapest ticket to not stir up suspicion. Many people would think a South American girl surely robbed a rich man to get the money for that ticket. Besides, I had to be smart with money right now.

The train ride is two days. I can keep myself occupied for that long.

I thought about Nellie in New York and wondered if she is excited to see me, or dreads having to keep a houseguest. I've heard a saying from one of the men at Pemberton's parties, "Houseguests are like fish. After three days, they start to stink!" Cue the forced laughter. I didn't want to overstay my welcome. Besides, I need to get home to Mama and Papa before Pemberton's men realize I'm missing. I decide to calm my worries with a book, this time fiction. Now that I have seemingly read every medical textbook known to man, I want to experience a different kind of pleasure from reading. I picked up Nathaniel Hawthorne's *The Scarlet Letter* from a bookstore a while ago. It's about a lady who commits a sin, sleeping with a man before marriage and having a baby, and is subjected to public humiliation and ostracization from her society for the rest of her life. Is that what I am to become? An outsider, in my own society? I wonder if the people in town will talk when I get back, if I get back. Will they applaud my efforts, or will they look at me in disgust because I failed. I abandoned my country, my heritage, to make something of myself. When the money and the money man fell through, so did I. Maybe they ought to put a scarlet letter on me so that everyone will know that I am a traitor to my own society.

The tears start to flow. I cannot help it. Every frustration and kept secret began to pour out of me. It's like when you climb a mountain, and you keep getting mislead by the peaks. You think you're at the top, but then another mountain appears practically out of thin air. There is nothing more frustrating than Mother Nature mocking you. *Ha, ha. You insignificant being. There's still so much more to go.* And you must accept it, because there is no fight when She is involved. Nature is unforgiving. She is what she is, and there is no alteration or human invention that can stop Her will to survive.

After two days of sitting my back and thighs ache. My buttocks is practically numb. I am so grateful when they call my stop. I hope Nellie is happy to see me. As I deboard the train, I am prepared to haul my way to Nellie's apartment, not knowing how far or what modes of transportation I would have to take to get there. But, to my surprise, she is standing at the visitor's platform. She looks the same as the day I met her on the ship, except a small bump extrudes from her stomach, and she has a nice glow to her face. My shoulders drop in relief and I heave out a big sigh that is caught in my throat with a sob. I run to her and throw my arms around her.

"No one's been that excited to see me in years." She laughs and throws her arms around me as well.

"Thank you, oh, thank you, Nellie. You've saved me."

"You must have had a long trip. Let's get you to a bed."

New York is even busier than Atlanta. The part Nellie lives in is mainly Irish and German immigrants. They work in factories, men and women, and their large families live in small, crowded apartments. Besides the stares, the city life up North seems exciting. Always something going on, always something to do.

"Here she is." Nellie whips out a key after we both climbed about six flights of stairs. She unlocks the apartment door and gestures me to enter in front of her.

"Lucila, this is me husband, me children, you met Niall when he was a wee baby, me daughter Eire, cousins, and their many offspring." I quickly count nine people in this tiny apartment.

"Good to meet 'ya, Lucila." Nellie's husband offers. The rest of them smile and quickly return to their individual activities.

"Do ye like beef stew? 'Cause that's what's fer dinner!" Nellie exclaims.

"Sounds wonderful."

I'm staying with Nellie for a week or so. There were no ships departing from Atlanta for at least a month, and surely Pemberton will be dead by then. From New York, however, there are always boats and ships and trains coming in and out. I leave tomorrow. During my stay, I tried to make myself as invisible as possible. I washed the dishes, offered to help cook, but mostly stayed out of the apartment, careful not to disturb their routines. Nellie works most of the day, as does her husband. Her cousin watches the children all day, while her other cousin sews dresses and sells them to local shops. It looks like a busy life, but fulfilling life. Their family is always together, and they get by just fine.

The ship departs today at noon. It will be another long voyage alone. But this time, I am filled with the world's knowledge. I have seen America and experienced her way of life. I have seen sadness and sorrow that is unspeakable, and I feel as though I have lived a full life there. Sometimes the greatest journeys we must experience alone, for that is the only way we can grow. I wonder how much Mama and Papa have changed. If they are still the same caring, loving people that raised me. I fear secretly that they resent me for leaving, failing, and suddenly returning with no clear explanation. I will explain everything when I return. But, before I go, I slip an envelope under Nellie's pillow with a quarter of my earnings from Pemberton's factory. It should be enough for her to stop working for a while when she has her baby.

I board the ship at noon and brace myself for an uneventful few weeks. But, for now, I prefer the uneventful. It reminds me that there is so much possibility in the future. I can go home. I can give Mama and Papa the money that they so desperately need. We can be a family again.

Epilogue
1890

Before I go, I'd like to give the reader one piece of advice. Find love; it makes the hard times less hard. When I returned back to Peru, one of the first people I saw was a familiar face. As soon as he swept his floppy hair out of his eyes, I knew who he was. Suddenly, he didn't seem so mischievous, so immature. He spoke with the best of intentions and won me over. Javier and I were married on September 21st, 1889. Mama loved planning the wedding. She made my dress, too. Papa, of course, drank too much wine and had too much fun. We all did.

I live in Lima, now, with Mama, Papa, and Javier. We got out of that small town when we heard that Charles and Mr. Byrd were looking for me. San Marcos had heard that I was the first Peruvian woman to go to medical school, let alone in America. They offered me a teaching job in pharmaceutical science. It's funny to see the students' reactions when I walk into the room. They can't believe I am their instructor! Soon, it will not be so strange. I'm starting a scholarship for women who want to pursue a career in the agricultural, biological, or chemical sciences. They can have the same chance that I did, but closer to home.

Pemberton never found me. He died in 1888, after he sold the company. None of the shareholders received the money, except his son. I'd like to think that Mr. Byrd finally spoke his truth to Pemberton before he passed. After Pemberton died, the company actually did fairly well. They were making a good profit under the new ownership. I knew the drink was good, but it never occurred to me that maybe Pemberton was the problem.

I live a happy life now. While I am still young and there is still so much to see, I am content from the past experiences and what it has led me to. I think about America sometimes, and I fear for its future. America is hungry for money and success, but I don't think America will ever be satisfied, no matter how much it consumes. Even though it is the place where people go to start anew, there is something lacking within the people there. Their morality is tainted, and the worth of a person is determined by a monetary and social scale. There's no fun, no playfulness in it at all. While I learned a lot about people, I now know that this is where I belong.

As I look out into the city from our apartment, I cradle my pregnant belly. The baby is unexpected, but not unwelcomed. I figure she will have enough family to be entertained, with Mama and Papa living with us. It's funny how you expect life to move towards one direction, then it swerves and suddenly you're on another path, with no say in it at all. It's better to accept that then try to hold on to dear life for control. You will fail everytime, I almost did. I will teach my children the same. I think if it is a boy, I will name him Edward.

A girl, Nellie.

If you enjoyed this book, please leave a review on Amazon!

Check out our other

books available on

Amazon

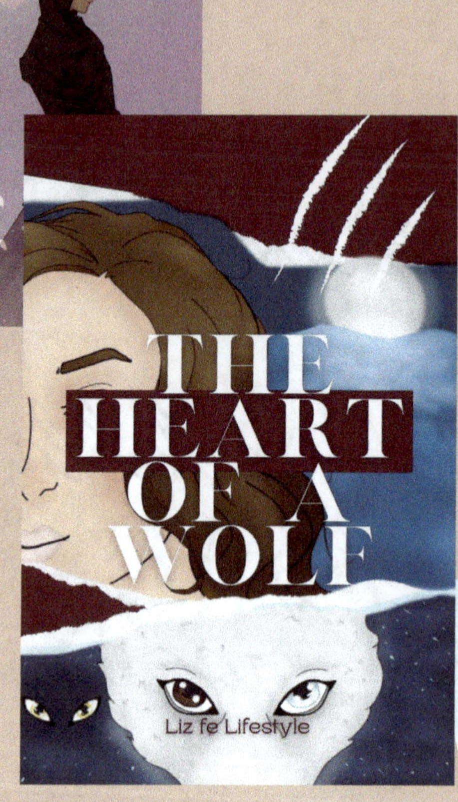

Secrets
from the
Mountaintop
LIZ FE LIFESTYLE
THE
HEART
OF A
WOLF
Liz fe Lifestyle
BEING
BORN
WITH A
RUSTY
SPOON
IN YOUR MOUTH
LIZ FE LIFESTYLE